NIX THE TRICKS

Second Edition

by

Tina Cardone and the MTBoS

Updated: October 24, 2015

i

ISBN: 978-1507504376

All student work was collected by classroom teachers during the course of regular lessons, then submitted to MathMistakes.org. To protect the privacy of students (and in many cases to improve legibility), each example was rewritten in the author's handwriting.

"I would say, then, that it is not reasonable to even mention this technique. If it is so limited in its usefulness, why grant it the privilege of a name and some memory space? Cluttering heads with specialized techniques that mask the important general principle at hand does the students no good, in fact it may harm them. Remember the Hippocratic oath – First, do no harm."

– Jim Doherty

Contents

Preface   viii

1   Introduction   1

2   Operations   5

   2.1   Nix: Total Means Add   5

   2.2   Nix: Bigger Bottom, Better Borrow   6

   2.3   Nix: Add a Zero (Multiplying by 10)   7

   2.4   Nix: Five or More Go up a Floor, aka 0-4 Hit the Floor, 5-9 Make the Climb   8

   2.5   Nix: Turtle Multiplication   9

   2.6   Nix: Does McDonald's Sell Cheeseburgers, a.k.a. Dad, Mom, Sister, Brother   10

   2.7   Nix: Ball to the Wall   11

   2.8   Nix: PEMDAS, BIDMAS   12

3   Proportional Reasoning   14

   3.1   Nix: Butterfly Method, Jesus Fish   15

   3.2   Nix: The Man on the Horse   16

   3.3   Nix: Make Mixed Numbers MAD   17

   3.4   Nix: Backflip and Cartwheel   18

   Cross Multiply   20

3.5   Nix: Cross Multiply
(Fraction Division)   21

3.6   Nix: Flip and Multiply,
Same-Change-Flip   24

3.7   Nix: Cross Multiply
(Solving Proportions)   24

3.8   Nix: Dr. Pepper   26

3.9   Nix: New Formulas for Each Conversion   . .   28

3.10   Nix: Formula Triangle   30

3.11   Nix: Outers over Inners   31

4   Geometry and Measurement   33

4.1   Nix: Perimeter is the Outside   33

4.2   Nix: Rectangles Have Two Long Sides and
Two Short Sides   34

4.3   Nix: Squares Have Four Equal Sides   34

4.4   Nix: Obtuse Angles are Big   35

4.5   Nix: $a^2 + b^2 = c^2$ 36

4.6   Nix: The Angle of Inclination Is the Same as
the Angle of Depression   37

Formulas   39

4.7   Formula: Areas of Quadrilaterals, Triangles   39

4.8   Formula: Surface Area   40

4.9   Formula: Volume   41

4.10   Formula: Distance Formula   42

5   Number Systems   43

5.1   Nix: Absolute Value Makes a Number Positive   43

5.2   Nix: Same-Change-Change,
Keep-Change-Change
(Integer Addition)   44

5.3   Nix: Two Negatives Make a Positive (Integer
Subtraction)   45

5.4   Nix: Two Negatives Make a Positive (Integer Multiplication) 47

5.5   Nix: Move the Decimal (Scientific Notation) 49

5.6   Nix: Jailbreak Radicals, aka You Need a Partner to Go to the Party 50

5.7   Nix: Exponent Over Radical 51

6   Equations and Inequalities   53

6.1   Nix: 'Hungry' Inequality Symbols 53

6.2   Nix: Take or Move to the Other Side 54

6.3   Nix: Switch the Side and Switch the Sign 55

6.4   Nix: Cancel 56

6.5   Nix: Follow the Arrow (Graphing Inequalities) 57

6.6   Nix: The Square Root and the Square Cancel   58

6.7   Nix: Land of Gor 59

6.8   Nix: Log Circle 61

6.9   Nix: The Log and the Exponent Cancel 61

7   Functions   64

7.1   Nix: Rise over Run as the Definition of Slope   64

7.2   Nix: OK vs. NO Slope 65

7.3   Nix: What is b? 66

7.4   Nix: The Inside Does the Opposite 67

7.5   Nix: All Students Take Calculus a.k.a CAST   69

7.6   Nix: FOIL 69

7.7   Nix: Slide and Divide, aka Throw the Football   72

7.8   Nix: Synthetic Division 75

8   Conclusion   77

A Index of Tricks by Standards   **82**

B Types of Tricks   **86**

    B.1 Imprecise Language 86

    B.2 Methods Eliminating Options 87

    B.3 Tricks Students Misinterpret 87

    B.4 Math as Magic, Not Logic 88

Preface

In the beginning, there was a calculus teacher complaining about students' lack of a definition of slope. Then there was a conversation among my department members on tricks we hate seeing kids show up to our classes with. I expanded the conversation to members of my online math community. We brainstormed and debated what constituted a trick and which were the worst offenders. I organized. More people joined in on the conversation and shared better methods to emphasize understanding over memorization. I organized some more. Contributions started to slow down. The end result was 17 pages in a Google Doc. I had grand dreams of a beautifully formatted resource that we could share with teachers everywhere. A few people shared my dream. We discussed formatting and organization and themes. Finally, inspired by NaNoWriMo, I opened up LaTeX and started typesetting. I got some help. This document was born. I hope you enjoy it all the more knowing how many people's ideas are encapsulated here.

2nd Edition: This project began in January of 2013. It is now November of 2014 and I cannot begin to describe the experience thus far. While my primary focus is still teaching, (full time at a high need public school in Massachusetts) this side project has allowed me to make connections with educators all over the world and pushed me to think deeply about mathematics at all levels. The Google Doc of new tricks for review has again grown to 16 pages. Not to mention the additional pages for vocabulary and notation. Once again inspired by NaNoWriMo I am taking the month to organize, edit, format and publish the second edition. In the meantime, more people than I could hope to thank have contributed to *Nix the Tricks* in countless ways. Here are just a few of the many people to whom I owe the existence of this text.

Thanks to all contributors:

Chuck Baker	High School Math Teacher @chuckcbaker, mrcbaker.blogger.com
Ashli Black	NBCT, Mathematics Consultant @mythagon, mythagon.wordpress.com
Tim Cieplowski	@timteachesmath
Jim Doherty	High School Math, Department Chair @mrdardy, mrdardy.wordpress.com
Mary Dooms	Middle School Math @mary_dooms, teacherleaders.wordpress.com
Nik Doran	
Bridget Dunbar	Math Instructional Resource Teacher - Middle School elsdunbar.wordpress.com
Michael Fenton	Nix the Tricks Editor in Chief, Mathematics Teacher, Consultant @mjfenton, reasonandwonder.com
Paul Flaherty	High School Math Teacher
Peggy Frisbie	High School Math Teacher
Emmanuel Garcia	
Marc Garneau	K-12 Numeracy Helping Teacher @314Piman, diaryofapiman.wordpress.com
John Golden	Math Ed Professor @mathhombre, mathhombre.blogspot.com
Megan Hayes-Golding	High School Math/Science Teacher
Chris Hill	Physics Teacher in Milwaukee @hillby258, hillby.wordpress.com
Scott Hills	
Chris Hlas	
Chris Hunter	K-12 Numeracy Helping Teacher @ChrisHunter36, reflectionsinthewhy.wordpress.com
Bowen Kerins	Senior Curriculum Writer cmeproject.edc.org

Rachel Kernodle	High School Math Teacher
Yvonne Lai	
Bob Lochel	High School Math @bobloch, mathcoachblog.com
TR Milne	High School Math
Jonathan Newman	High School Math/Science hilbertshotel.wordpress.com
Kate Nowak	MTBoS High Priestess function-of-time.blogspot.com
Jami Packer	High School Special Education @jamidanielle, jamidanielle.blogspot.com
Jim Pai	High School Math @PaiMath, intersectpai.blogspot.ca
Michael Pershan	Elementary/High School Math Teacher @mpershan, rationalexpressions.blogspot.com
Avery Pickford	Middle School Math @woutgeo, withoutgeometry.com
Julie Reulbach	Middle/High School Math Teacher
Gabe Rosenberg	High School/College Math Teacher
Mark Sanford	High School Math Teacher
Sam Shah	High School Math Teacher samjshah.com
Jack Siderer	
Gregory Taylor	High School Math Teacher @mathtans
Sue VanHattum	Math Professor, Editor, Playing with Math mathmamawrites.blogspot.com
Lane Walker	NBCT, High School Math @LaneWalker2
Lim Wei Quan	
Julie Wright	Middle School Math Teacher @msjwright2, sadarmadillo.blogspot.com
Mimi Yang	Middle/High School Math Teacher @untilnextstop
Amy Zimmer	

and many more who chose to remain anonymous.

Each chapter follows a concept thread. For example, you might see how content knowledge should build from drawing representations of fractions to solving proportions. Feel free to read this as a book, from front to back, or jump directly to those sections that apply to your grade level of interest (see the Index to find the tricks organized by Common Core Standard).

Chapter 1

Introduction

This text is inspired by committed teachers who want to take the magic out of mathematics and focus on the beauty of sense-making. It is written for reflective teachers who embrace the Common Core Standards for Mathematical Practice. The contributors are people who wish for teachers everywhere to seek coherence and connection rather than offer students memorized procedures and short-cutting tricks. Students are capable of developing rich conceptual understanding; do not rob them of the opportunity to experience the discovery of new concepts.

This is a hard step to take; students will have to think and they will say they do not want to. Students (and parents and tutors) will need to readjust their expectations, however, it is in the best interest of students everywhere to make the focus of mathematics critical thinking. Will you help math reclaim its position as a creative and thought-provoking subject?

"But it's just to help them remember - I taught them the concept!"

SOH CAH TOA is a mnemonic device. There is no underlying reason why sine is the ratio of opposite to hypotenuse; it is a definition. Kids can use this abbreviation without losing any understanding.

FOIL is a trick. There is a good reason why we multiply binomials in a certain way, and this acronym circumvents student understanding of the power and flexibility of the distributive property. If you teach the distributive property, ask students to develop their own shortcut and then give it a name; that is awesome. However, the phrase "each by each" is more powerful than FOIL since it does not imply that a certain order is necessary (my honors precalculus students were shocked to hear OLIF would work just as well as FOIL) and reminds students of what they are doing. Many students will wait for the shortcut and promptly forget the reasoning behind it if the trick comes too soon or from a place beyond their current understanding.

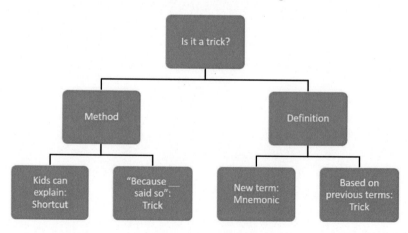

A trick is magic; something kids understand is a shortcut or rule. If they can explain the process it loses trick status – not all shortcuts are bad. The book's subtitle is key: "A guide to avoiding shortcuts that cut out math concept development." When in doubt, check for student understanding.

"My students can't understand the higher level math, but they do great with the trick."

If students do not understand, they are not doing math. Do not push students too far, too fast (adolescent brains need time to develop before they can truly comprehend abstraction), but do not sell your students short either. The world does not need more robots; asking children to mindlessly follow an algorithm is not teaching them anything more than how to follow instructions. There are a million ways to teach reading and following directions; do not reduce mathematics to that single skill. Allow students to experience and play and notice and wonder. They will surprise you! Being a mathematician is not limited to rote memorization (though learning the perfect squares by heart will certainly help one to recognize that structure). Being a mathematician is about critical thinking, justification and using tools of past experiences to solve new problems. Being a successful adult involves pattern finding, questioning others and perseverance. Focus on these skills and allow students to grow into young adults who can think – everything else will come in time.

"This is all well and good, but we don't have enough TIME!"

Yes, this approach takes an initial investment of time. I would argue that we should push back against the testing pressure rather than push back against concept development, but that is a whole other book. First, if we teach concepts rather than tricks, students will retain more. Each year will start with less confusion of "keep-change-change or keep-keep-change?" and any associated misconceptions, which means each year will have more time for new content. Second, teachers have to make tough choices all the time, and choosing between depth and breadth is a major choice. Every year my department gets together and tries to guess which topics in Geometry are least likely to be on the state test. We leave those topics for after the exam and do our very best to teach the other topics well. If students go into the test with solid reasoning skills they will at the very least be able to determine which choices are reasonable, if not reason all the way through an inscribed angle problem (circles usually lose our lottery).

Read through these pages with an open mind. Consider how you can empower students to discover a concept and find their own shortcuts (complete with explanations!). I do not ask you to blindly accept these pages as the final authority any more than I would ask students to blindly trust teachers. Engage with the content and discover the best teaching approaches for your situation. Share and discuss with your colleagues. Ask questions, join debates and make suggestions at NixTheTricks.com.

Chapter 2

Operations

2.1 Nix: Total Means Add

Because:

Total → Add
Left → Subtract
Each → Multiply
Shared → Divide

Context matters. The phrase 'in all' means different things in "Tina has 3 cookies, Chris has 5, how many cookies are there *in all*?" and "Cookies come in bags of 15. If you buy 3 bags of cookies, how many cookies do you have *in all*?" Students will lose their sense making skills, and their belief that math makes sense, if the focus is on circling and crossing out words.

Fix:

Instead of teaching a few key words, ask students to think about all the words and what is happening. Have students draw a model of the situation rather than jumping directly to the computation. Kids are able to reason through problems, especially in story problems where students have experiences they can apply to the context. Encourage students to use their sense-making skills (which they arrive to school with) both in figuring out the problem, and in checking the reasonableness of their answer. As a bonus, students will simultaneously develop their reading comprehension skills. Start with the mantra "math makes sense" and never let kids believe anything else.

2.2 Nix: Bigger Bottom, Better Borrow

Because:

This trick has students sidestep thinking. They do not look at the numbers as a whole or reason about what subtraction means.

$$23$$
$$-1\cancel{8}$$

Fix:

Students must understand subtraction as a concept and as an operation before the rules of an algorithm can make sense to them. If we try to push the algorithm before that understanding is solid, then we force students to go against their intuition (for instance, the intuition that says you always subtract the smaller number). When we ask children to follow a procedure that holds no meaning for them, they will conclude that math does not make sense. Go back to the mantra "math makes sense" and make sure all students believe it when they learn the subtraction algorithm.

To achieve this: Start with adding/subtracting within 10, then within 20, then multiples of 10. Combining these skills allows students to understand subtraction with regrouping. When adding and subtracting any pair of expressions (algebraic or otherwise), we must add and subtract "like terms." For terms to be alike, they must have the same place value.

6

$\begin{array}{r} 23 \\ -\ 9 \\ \hline \end{array}$

$\begin{array}{r} {\scriptstyle 1} \\ \cancel{2}3 \\ -\ 9 \\ \hline \end{array}$

$\begin{array}{r} {\scriptstyle 1} \\ \cancel{2}3 \\ -\ 9 \\ \hline 14 \end{array}$

When subtracting 9 from 23, there are only three ones, and so we regroup into 13 ones and a ten. Before students can make this regrouping mentally they need to experience it – with manipulatives such as ten frames and unit cubes. With enough practice, students will begin to do the computation without needing to count out each piece. At this point they will be ready for the abstraction of an algorithm.

2.3 Nix: Add a Zero (Multiplying by 10)

Because:
$$10 \cdot 10 = 100$$

When students study integers, multiplying by 10 means to "add a zero," but once they head into the realm of real numbers the phrase changes to "move the decimal point." Neither phrase conveys any meaning about multiplication or place value. "Add a zero" should mean "add the additive identity" which does not change the value at all!

Fix:

Have students multiply by ten just like they multiply by any other number. When a student discovers a pattern: first congratulate them for noticing and sharing, then ask them whether they think their pattern will always work. If they believe it does generalize, ask them why their rule works. Finally, if the student can justify their pattern for a particular situation, remind them to be careful about mindlessly applying it in novel situations (ask them about $10 \cdot 0$ for example). One way to help students see why their pattern works is to use a place value chart to show what is happening: each of the ones becomes a ten $(1 \cdot 10 = 10)$, each of the tens becomes a hundred $(10 \cdot 10 = 100)$, etc. The pattern of shifting place value works all up and down the decimal scale. You could name the pattern, "Student A's rule for multiplying by 10" if you want to be able to refer back to it.

2.4 Nix: Five or More Go up a Floor, aka 0-4 Hit the Floor, 5-9 Make the Climb

Because:

$$3.\!\!\;\textcircled{4}\!\downarrow$$
$$5.2\textcircled{4}\textcircled{9}\uparrow$$

When using this trick students do not realize that rounding means choosing the closest number at the indicated place value. This means that they do not understand what to do, for example, with the ones place if they are rounding to the hundreds place. Students are able to tell what is closer without a rhyme and deserve a reason why we choose to round up with five.

Fix:

Begin the study of rounding using number lines so students can see which number is closer. The problem is that five is not closer to either side; it is exactly in the middle (as long as it is a five with nothing but zeros after it). We have to make a rule for which way we are going to round five, because it could go either way. The convention in math

8

class is to round up, which makes sense if you consider that there are often non-zero digits in the place values after the 5. For example, 253 is closer to 300 than to 200 even though 250 is equidistant between the two.

2.5 Nix: Turtle Multiplication

Because:

The cute story only serves to overload the students' minds and distracts them from the task at hand – multiplication.

Fix:

Just as with any other algorithm, students need to build up their understanding so the procedure is not something to be memorized, but rather a quick way to record a series of steps that make sense. Students should build their understanding using area models, followed by partial products. When students can compute partial products fluently they are ready for the abbreviated version (the standard algorithm).

	20	3
5	100	15

$$23 \cdot 5 = (20 + 3) \cdot 5$$
$$= 20 \cdot 5 + 3 \cdot 5$$
$$= 100 + 15$$
$$= 115$$

2.6 Nix: Does McDonald's Sell Cheeseburgers, a.k.a. Dad, Mom, Sister, Brother

Because:

Students should understand the process, not memorize a procedure. Not to mention the fact that it is just as hard to remember the order of the family members in this arbitrary mnemonic as it would be to remember arbitrary operations. Describing the process without understanding leads to confusion; what mathematical operation is equivalent to 'bring down the 2?'

$$
\begin{array}{r}
1 \\
7\overline{)823} \\
-71 \\
\hline
12
\end{array}
\quad
\begin{array}{l}
\text{Divide} \\
\text{Multiply} \\
\text{Subtract} \\
\text{Bring} \\
\text{Down}
\end{array}
$$

Fix:

Students cannot see place value when using the standard algorithm for dividing. Adding some color and writing out the entire number helps make the process more transparent. So does allowing students to take away less than the maximum amount each time - students will learn that the process goes faster if they maximize at each step, but there is no harm in taking two steps to do something if it helps students feel more confident.

$$
\begin{array}{r}
7 \\
10 \\
100
\end{array}
\left.\right\} 117\ R4
$$

$$
\begin{array}{r}
7\overline{)823} \\
-700 \\
\hline
123 \\
-\ 70 \\
\hline
53 \\
-\ 49 \\
\hline
4
\end{array}
$$

2.7 Nix: Ball to the Wall

Because:

Students have no idea why they are moving the decimal point, which means they are likely to misinterpret this rule and think that $5.5 \div 2.5 = 5.5 \div 25$ rather than the correct statement $5.5 \div 2.5 = 55 \div 25$.

Fix:

If a number has digits after the decimal point, this means there is only part of a whole. Since it is easier to work with whole numbers when dividing, we can write a different question that would have the same solution. Consider $10 \div 5$ and $100 \div 50$. These have the same solution because they are proportional:

$$\frac{10}{5} = \frac{10}{5} \cdot 1 \qquad\qquad \frac{10.3}{5.2} = \frac{10.3}{5.2} \cdot 1$$

$$= \frac{10}{5} \cdot \frac{10}{10} \qquad\qquad = \frac{10.3}{5.2} \cdot \frac{10}{10}$$

$$= \frac{10 \cdot 10}{5 \cdot 10} \qquad\qquad = \frac{10.3 \cdot 10}{5.2 \cdot 10}$$

$$= \frac{100}{50} \qquad\qquad\qquad = \frac{103}{52}$$

More generally, $\frac{x}{y} = \frac{10x}{10y}$, so $x \div y = (10x) \div (10y)$. It is interesting to note that multiplying by 10 is not the only option, any equivalent ratio with a whole number divisor will work for long division.

2.8 Nix: PEMDAS, BIDMAS

Because:

Students interpret the acronym in the
order the letters are presented, leading
them to multiply before dividing and add before subtracting.

$$PEMDAS$$
$$(\ )\verb|^| * / + -$$

For example, students often incorrectly evaluate $6 \div 2 \cdot 5$ as follows:

$$\text{Incorrect: } 6 \div 2 \cdot 5 = 6 \div 10 = 0.6$$

$$\text{Correct: } 6 \div 2 \cdot 5 = \frac{6}{2} \cdot 5 = 3 \cdot 5 = 15$$

Fix:

Students should know that mathematicians needed a standard order of operations for consistency. The most powerful operations should be completed first – exponentiation increases or decreases at a greater rate than multiplying, which increases or decreases at a greater rate than addition. Sometimes we want to use a different order, so we use grouping symbols to signify "do this first" when it is not the most powerful operation. If students are still looking for a way to remember the order, replace the confusing acronym PEMDAS with the clearer GEMA.

G is for grouping, which is better than parentheses because it includes all types of groupings such as brackets, absolute value, expressions under radicals (for example, square roots), the numerator of a fraction, etc. Grouping also implies more than one item, which eliminates the confusion students experience when they try to "Do the parentheses first." in $4(3)$.

E is for exponents. This includes radicals as they can be rewritten as exponents.

M is for multiplication. Division is implied. Since only one letter appears for both operations, it is essential to emphasize the important inverse relationship between multiplication and division. For example, discuss the equivalence of dividing by a fraction and multiplying by its reciprocal.

A is for addition. Subtraction is implied. Again, since only one letter appears for both operations, it is essential to emphasize the important inverse relationship between addition and subtraction. A useful definition for subtract is "add the opposite."

Chapter 3

Proportional Reasoning

Ratios and proportions are a new way of thinking for elementary students. Teachers often bemoan the difficulty that kids have with fractions, but students struggle because we rob them of the opportunity to develop any intuition with proportional reasoning. The first experience most people have with math is counting, then adding, along with additive patterns. Even when students start multiplying, it tends to be defined as repeated addition. Fractions are the first time when additive reasoning will not work, and it messes students up. Skip the shortcuts and let your kids see that fractions, ratios and proportions are multiplicative - a whole new way to interpret the world!

3.1 Nix: Butterfly Method, Jesus Fish

Because:

Students have no idea why it works and there is no mathematical reasoning behind the butterfly, no matter how pretty it is.

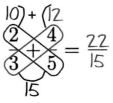

Fix:

If students start with visuals such as fraction strips they will discover the need to have like terms before they can add. Say a student wants to add $\frac{1}{2} + \frac{1}{4}$. They may start with a representation of each fraction, then add the fractions by placing them end to end. The representation is valid, but there is no way to translate this new diagram into a single fraction. To do so, students need to cut the whole into equal parts. After some

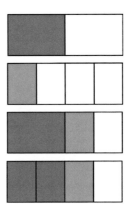

experience, students will realize they need common denominators to add. After still more experience adding fractions with common denominators, students will realize they can simply add the numerators (which is equivalent to counting the number of shaded pieces) while keeping the denominator the same (as the size of the pieces does not change).

Fractions can be compared and added or subtracted with any common denominator; there is no mathematical reason to limit students to the least common denominator. Many visual/manipulative methods will not give least common denominators (instead using the product of the denominators) and that is just fine! Accept any denominator that is computationally accurate. Students may eventually gravitate towards the least common denominator as they look for the easiest numbers to work with. In the meantime, encourage students to compare different methods – do different common denominators give different answers? Are they really different or might they be equivalent? How did that happen? Fractions can even be compared with common numerators – a fascinating discussion to have with students of any age!

3.2   Nix: The Man on the Horse

Trick Explanation:
The fraction is 'a man on a horse.' The man on the horse goes inside the house, but the horse must remain outside the house.

Because:

The fact that the dividend is the numerator when they set up the problem to divide should not be something students need help remembering. Plus, students are thrown off when there is a case where the man (numerator) is larger than the horse (denominator) because that makes even less sense!

Fix:

The notation used for fractions is not entirely foreign if students have been using either $\div$ or $/$ for division. The fraction line is just like each of these, except now we read top to bottom rather than left to right. Instead of introducing

16

fraction division as a new concept, share that the fraction line is merely another way to write 'divided by.'

3.3   Nix: Make Mixed Numbers MAD

Because:

$$3^{+1}_{\times 5} \overset{3\times 5 + 1}{MAD} \overset{16}{5}$$

This shortcut allows students to convert a mixed number to an improper fraction without understanding how wholes relate to fractions. This process skips the important conceptual steps that are happening behind the scenes.

Fix:

To show that $3\frac{1}{5} = \frac{16}{5}$, students should know that each whole is equal to $\frac{5}{5}$. This process should begin with manipulatives and diagrams so that students see that a whole is a fraction where the numerator is equal to the denominator. Students also need to know that common denominators are necessary to add fractions. Once both of those concepts have been developed, combine the two ideas to convert the whole numbers into fractions with common denominators:

$$3\frac{1}{5} = 1 + 1 + 1 + \frac{1}{5}$$

$$= \frac{5}{5} + \frac{5}{5} + \frac{5}{5} + \frac{1}{5}$$

$$= \frac{16}{5}$$

After students have repeated this process many times they will be able to go from $3\frac{1}{5}$ to $\frac{15}{5} + \frac{1}{5}$. Eventually they may be able to complete the entire computation mentally, but it is essential that students have the understanding of how to write one whole as a fraction to fall back on. Repeated practice converting the whole numbers to fractions with like denominators and only then adding the fractions will secure this concept in students' memories.

3.4 Nix: Backflip and Cartwheel

Because:

There is no reasoning involved in this trick and it is very easy to mix up. Cartwheels and backflips both involve flipping upside down in the middle; if one fraction gets flipped around, why not the other?

$$\frac{16}{5} \qquad 5\overline{)16}$$

$$3\frac{1}{5} \qquad 3 \times 5 + 1 \qquad \frac{16}{5}$$

Fix:

See Section 3.3 for converting mixed numbers to improper fractions.

To convert improper fractions to mixed numbers we should follow the same process in reverse. The goal is to remove as many wholes from the fraction as possible.

$$\frac{16}{5} = \frac{5}{5} + \frac{11}{5}$$

$$= \frac{5}{5} + \frac{5}{5} + \frac{6}{5}$$

$$= \frac{5}{5} + \frac{5}{5} + \frac{5}{5} + \frac{1}{5}$$

$$= 1 + 1 + 1 + \frac{1}{5}$$

$$= 3 + \frac{1}{5}$$

After students have repeated this process a few times they will begin to take out more than one whole at a time, going from $\frac{16}{5}$ to $\frac{15}{5} + \frac{1}{5}$ in one step.

Representing this process as division is also a valid approach. It will certainly help in transitioning to converting fractions to decimals. However, students should not need a trick to know that the denominator is the divisor. The denominator of a fraction tells how many parts to *divide* the whole into.

Cross Multiply

Kids want to use the phrase "Cross Multiply" for everything: How do we multiply fractions? "Cross Multiply!"
How do we divide fractions? "Cross Multiply!" How do
we solve proportions? "Cross Multiply!" Those are three
entirely different processes; they need different names. For
multiplication of fractions, 'Cross Multiply' means 'multiply
across' (horizontally), and there usually is not a trick associated with this operation. By high school most students
have no difficulty with this operation – it matches their intuition. In fact, they like this method so much they want
to extend it to other operations (non-example: to add fractions, add the numerators and add the denominators) a case
where students' intuition fails them. Instead of saying 'cross
multiply,' use the precise (though admittedly cumbersome)
phrase "multiply numerator by numerator and denominator
by denominator" when students need a reminder of how to
multiply fractions. To build upon and justify student intuition, direct students to an area model to determine the
product.

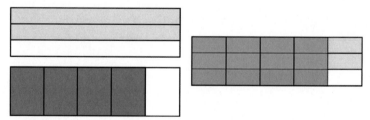

To multiply $\frac{2}{3} \cdot \frac{4}{5}$ find the area shaded by both – that
is two-thirds of four-fifths. The fifths are each divided into
thirds and two of the three are shaded. The resulting product is $\frac{8}{15}$.

3.5 Nix: Cross Multiply (Fraction Division)

$$\frac{2}{3} \div \frac{4}{5} = \frac{10}{12}$$

Because:

Division and multiplication are different (albeit related) operations; one cannot magically switch the operation in an expression. Plus, students confuse "cross" (diagonal) with "across" (horizontal). Not to mention, where does the answer go? Why does one product end up in the numerator and the other in the denominator?

Please, never tell students the phrase, "Ours is not to reason why; just invert and multiply." A student's job in math class is to reason, and a teacher's job is to convince the students that math makes sense.

Fix:

Use the phrase "multiply by the reciprocal," but only after students understand where this algorithm comes from. The reciprocal is a precise term that reminds students why we are switching the operation.

$$\frac{2}{3} \div \frac{2}{3} = 1 \quad \text{easy!}$$

$$\frac{2}{3} \div \frac{1}{3} = 2 \quad \text{makes sense}$$

$$\frac{4}{5} \div \frac{3}{5} = \frac{4}{3} \quad \text{not as obvious, but still dividing the numerators}$$

$$\frac{4}{5} \div \frac{1}{2} = ? \quad \text{no idea!}$$

If the last problem looked like the previous examples, it would be easier. So let's rewrite with common denominators:

$$\frac{8}{10} \div \frac{5}{10} = \frac{8}{5} \quad \text{makes sense}$$

If students are asked to solve enough problems in this manner, they will want to find a shortcut and may recognize the pattern. Show them (or ask them to prove!) why multiplying by the reciprocal works:

$$\frac{4}{5} \div \frac{1}{2} = \frac{4 \cdot 2}{5 \cdot 2} \div \frac{1 \cdot 5}{2 \cdot 5}$$

$$= \frac{4 \cdot 2}{1 \cdot 5} = \frac{4 \cdot 2}{5 \cdot 1}$$

$$= \frac{4}{5} \cdot \frac{2}{1}$$

In this case students discover that multiplying by the reciprocal is the equivalent of getting the common denominator and dividing the numerators. This is not an obvious fact. Students will only reach this realization with repeated practice, but practice getting common denominators is a great thing for them to be doing! More importantly, the student who forgets this generalization can fall back on an understanding of common denominators, while the student who learned a rule after completing this exercise once (or not at all!) will guess at the rule rather than attempt to reason through the problem.

A second approach uses compound fractions. Depending on what experience students have with reciprocals (say you want your older students to understand or prove the rule for dividing fractions), this might be a more friendly option. It has the added bonus of using a generalizable concept of multiplying by "a convenient form of one" which applies to many topics, including the application of unit conversions (Section 3.9). To begin, the division of two fractions can be written as one giant (complex or compound) fraction.

$$\frac{\frac{4}{5}}{\frac{1}{2}} = \frac{\frac{4}{5}}{\frac{1}{2}} \cdot 1$$

$$= \frac{\frac{4}{5}}{\frac{1}{2}} \cdot \frac{\frac{2}{1}}{\frac{2}{1}}$$

$$= \frac{\frac{4}{5} \cdot \frac{2}{1}}{1}$$

$$= \frac{4}{5} \cdot \frac{2}{1}$$

3.6 Nix: Flip and Multiply, Same-Change-Flip

Because:

$$\frac{2}{3} \div \frac{4}{5} = \frac{2}{3} \cdot \frac{5}{4}$$

Division and multiplication are different (albeit related) operations, one cannot magically switch the operation in an expression. Plus, students get confused as to what to "flip."

Fix:

Use the same methods as described in the fix of Section 3.5.

3.7 Nix: Cross Multiply (Solving Proportions)

Because:

Students confuse 'cross' (diagonal) with $2 \cdot 5 = x \cdot 3$ 'across' (horizontal) multiplication, and/or believe it can be used everywhere (such as in multiplication of fractions).

Correct multiplication of fractions: $\dfrac{1}{2} \cdot \dfrac{3}{4} = \dfrac{1 \cdot 3}{2 \cdot 4} = \dfrac{3}{8}$

Common error: $\dfrac{1}{2} \cdot \dfrac{3}{4} = \dfrac{1 \cdot 4}{2 \cdot 3} = \dfrac{4}{6}$

More importantly, you are not magically allowed to multiply two sides of an equation by different values to get an equivalent equation. This process does not make sense to students. They are memorizing a procedure, not understanding a method; which means that when they forget a step, they guess.

This student tries to multiply fractions using cross multiplication:

$$\frac{x^2 y^3}{m^4} \cdot \frac{m^2}{x^{-1} y^4}$$

$$x^2 y^3 \cdot x^1 y^4 = m^2 \cdot m^4$$

$$x' y^7 = m^6$$

http://mathmistakes.org/?p=476

This student uses cross addition instead of multiplication:

$$\frac{8x}{30} = \frac{48}{18}$$

$$26x = 78$$

$$\frac{26x}{26} \quad \frac{78}{26}$$

$$x = 3$$

http://mathmistakes.org/?p=1320

Fix:

Proportions are equivalent fractions. Encourage students to look for shortcuts such as common denominators or common numerators in addition to using scale factors. Once students know when and why a shortcut works, skipping a few steps is okay, but students must know why their shortcut is 'legal algebra' and have a universal method to fall back on.

$$\frac{3}{5} = \frac{x}{5} \Leftrightarrow x = 3$$

no work required, meaning of equal

$$\frac{3}{5} = \frac{x}{10} \Leftrightarrow \frac{3 \cdot 2}{5 \cdot 2} = \frac{x}{10}$$
$$\Leftrightarrow x = 6$$

multiply by 1 to get an equivalent fraction

$$\frac{4}{8} = \frac{x}{10} \Leftrightarrow x = 5$$

students recognize $\frac{1}{2}$ (any equivalent ratio works)

$$\frac{5}{3} = \frac{10}{x} \Leftrightarrow \frac{3}{5} = \frac{x}{10}$$

take the reciprocal of both sides of the equation

25

Proportions can also be approached as equations to solve. Instruct solving all equations (including proportions, they aren't special!) by inverse operations.

$$\frac{3}{5} = \frac{x}{10}$$

$$10 \cdot \frac{3}{5} = 10 \cdot \frac{x}{10}$$

$$10 \cdot \frac{3}{5} = x$$

$$6 = x$$

3.8   Nix: Dr. Pepper

Because:

D.P. 43.2%

Students do not need to know what a percent represents to use this method. Instead of magically moving the decimal point, use the definition of percent to interpret the number.

D.P. .42

Fix:

Percent means per 100. Students who know that percents are out of 100 can then write their percents as fractions. From there they can use knowledge of converting between fractions and decimals. No need to learn a new process (or magically move decimal points!). Percents are an excellent opportunity to work with students on understanding the connection between fractions and decimals. We read the number 0.54 as 54 hundredths, which means $\frac{54}{100}$, which is the definition of 54%. This does become slightly more complex if students have not seen decimals in fractions. In the case of 43.2% we know:

$$43.2\% = \frac{43.2}{100}$$
$$= \frac{43.2}{100} \cdot 1$$
$$= \frac{43.2}{100} \cdot \frac{10}{10}$$
$$= \frac{432}{1000}$$
$$= 0.432$$

Students should understand that 100% corresponds to one whole, so that percentages 0 - 100% correspond to decimal numbers between zero and one. There are also percents greather than 100, just as there are fractions greater than one.

Another approach is to multiply (or divide) by 100%. This is multiplying (or dividing) by 1, which does not change the value. Beware of students who will literally type 0.54 ∗ 100% into the calculator (there is a percent button on many scientific calculators) as this button is an operation not a label.

3.9 Nix: New Formulas for Each Conversion

$$d = rt \quad \text{(distance/time)}$$
$$s = r\theta \quad \text{(arc length)}$$
$$p = 100d \quad \text{(percent/decimal)}$$
$$i = ps \quad \text{(scale factor)}$$

Because:

All conversions are equivalent, regardless of units; there is no need to give them separate formulas to make students think they should be compartmentalized. Scale factor, percent, arc length and unit conversions all use the same strategies. The more connections students can make, the more solid their understanding will be.

Fix:

Talk about units. All the time. If students recognize how to use units then each of these situations will be a new unit to learn, but not a new procedure to learn. When teaching circles in precalculus, I assigned some problems on linear and angular speed. Most students in the class had taken chemistry and mastered unit conversions in that course, but it did not occur to them to apply that skill to this new context. We need to work with our science colleagues and use units regularly.

When students convert something, show them what they did. If there are 5 dozen eggs, students think they need to multiply $5 \cdot 12$. If we include the units the process becomes clearer: $5 \text{ dozen} \cdot \frac{12 \text{ eggs}}{1 \text{ dozen}}$. Teach students that they are multiplying by one – they have not changed the value (there are still the same number of eggs) but instead have changed the units (eggs vs. dozens). This will also help students avoid the problems that can be caused by key words (Section 2.1). If students stop thinking about what makes sense, they may randomly combine numbers that they are given. District math specialist, Robert Kaplin-sky, asked a class of eighth graders, "There are 125 sheep and 5 dogs in a flock. How old is the shepherd?" and **75%** of students gave a numerical answer. (Read more about his informal research: http://robertkaplinsky.com/how-old-is-the-shepherd/). When students do not see what is happening in early unit conversion situations, they stop paying attention to these important cues and focus solely on numbers. Units should not magically change – math makes sense.

Once they understand how to use units, students can learn to write equations in the form $y = kx$ where k is the constant of proportionality. Then students can identify conversions as a form of direct variation. To determine the constant of proportionality, students must recognize that a unit (of measure) is equivalent to a certain number of another unit: 1 foot $= 12$ inches. Then, conversion takes place by multiplying by 1, where the 1 is formed from the equivalency, such as $\frac{12 \text{ in}}{1 \text{ ft}}$. To help students get started, ask them what they know about the unit. For example, with radians, ask students what angle they know in both degrees and radians. They may tell you 2π radians $= 360$ degrees or π radians $= 180$ degrees. Then they have enough information to set up an equation.

Proportions are the same as direct variation; $y = kx$ is equivalent to $\frac{y}{x} = k$, so equations where k is a rational number are proportions. Direct variation equations place the emphasis on converting from input to output, while proportions show the equivalence of two comparisons more readily. The other benefit of direct variation is it is easy to expand. To convert several units (seconds to minutes to hours), extend the equation to $y = k_1 \cdot k_2 \cdot x$.

3.10 Nix: Formula Triangle

Trick Explanation:
To find distance, cover D in the triangle, r·t remains. To find rate, cover r in the triangle and you see $\frac{D}{t}$. To find time, cover t in the triangle, leaving $\frac{D}{r}$.

Because:

Covering up part of a triangle is not a valid method for solving an equation. Direct variation problems are no different than any other equation; use the same strategies.

Fix:

Students can use unit analysis (Section 3.9) to solve rate problems. It is perfectly reasonable to expect students to learn one equation, say $d = rt$, which is no harder to remember than the triangle. In fact, it is easier to write an equation since students can check that the units work if they forget; no such luck with the triangle. Once they know one equation they can use opposite operations to manipulate it. This process involves much more sense making than setting up a new expression for each variable without any understanding of how the parts of the triangle relate.

To find out how a middle school math teacher, David Cox, engaged his students in a discussion when they brought up this trick, see the conclusion.

3.11   Nix: Outers over Inners

Because:

Students have no idea what they are doing, so chances are not good that they will remember the difference between inners over outers and outers over inners. It seems arbitrary and has no connection to the mathematical operation of division. Remember, math makes sense.

$$\left(\frac{\dfrac{x}{3}}{\dfrac{5x}{9}}\right) \quad \frac{9x}{15x}$$

Fix:

Complex fractions are, well, complex. Students who know how to both divide fractions and simplify expressions get lost in the cognitive overload of variables combined with fractions! These problems do not have to be a student's worst nightmare, though. While these fractions look more complicated, they work just like any other fraction. One way to divide fractions is to multiply by the reciprocal (Section 3.5). That works well when both the numerator and denominator are single fractions. Another approach, that is more versatile, is to multiply by the common denominator, similar to the first proof of Cross Multiply: Fraction Division (Section 3.5).

$$\frac{2 + \frac{x}{3}}{4 + \frac{6x}{9}} = \frac{2 + \frac{x}{3}}{4 + \frac{6x}{9}} \cdot \frac{9}{9}$$

$$= \frac{18 + 3x}{36 + 6x}$$

$$= \frac{3(6 + x)}{6(6 + x)}$$

$$= \frac{3}{6} = \frac{1}{2}$$

$$\frac{2 + \frac{3}{2x}}{4 - \frac{5}{3x^2}} = \frac{2 + \frac{3}{2x}}{4 - \frac{5}{3x^2}} \cdot \frac{6x^2}{6x^2}$$

$$= \frac{12x^2 + 9x}{24x^2 - 10}$$

$$= \frac{3x(4x + 3)}{2(12x^2 - 5)}$$

Students would do well to refer back to how they would solve a simpler problem. Once students have found a common denominator, simplifying the numerator and the denominator separately can help students avoid the temptation to 'cancel' (Section 6.4) terms before factoring.

Chapter 4

Geometry and Measurement

4.1 Nix: Perimeter is the Outside

Because:

Students interpret this to mean all the space outside a shape rather than the edge. The description should tell students what the units are (length vs. area).

Fix:

The definition of perimeter is "The distance around a shape." It is important to emphasize that it is a distance, so students know they are looking for a one dimensional answer. This helps students who cannot remember the difference between $2\pi r$ and πr^2. The first is one dimensional (r) and measures distance – perimeter/circumference. The other is two dimensional (r^2) and measures area. Students do not need to memorize formulas for the perimeter of polygons. They can be encouraged to find shortcuts for computational ease (notice that all the sides of the square are the same length so they could multiply by four) but if a student forgets how to find perimeter they should fall back on the definition rather than looking up a formula.

4.2 Nix: Rectangles Have Two Long Sides and Two Short Sides

Because:

A rectangle is not a stretched out square. Rather, a square is a special rectangle. This means that the set of rectangles needs to be a broader category with squares as a subset. Describing a rectangle as a shape with two long sides and two short sides excludes squares and includes parallelograms.

Fix:

The definition of a rectangle is "A quadrilateral with four right angles." That is it! There does not need to be any mention of sides, just angles. In the proper hierarchy: rectangles are equiangular quadrilaterals, rhombi are equilateral quadrilaterals and squares are both/regular.

4.3 Nix: Squares Have Four Equal Sides

Because:

This is the definition of a rhombus. This definition does not adequately describe a square.

Fix:

Use the definition: "A quadrilateral with four equal sides AND four equal angles." Alternatively, "A rectangle with four equal sides" is an excellent description of a square as it emphasizes the square as a subset of rectangles.

4.4   Nix: Obtuse Angles are Big

Because:

When students hear the words big or large they are thinking about something taking up a large amount of space. So students see small and large as describing the length of the ray rather than the degree measure.

Fix:

The definition of obtuse is "An angle with measure between 90 and 180 degrees." When explaining this definition or describing angles use 'wide angle' not 'large angle.' Wide vs. narrow fits the hinge model of an angle and focuses student attention on the space between the rays – the angle – rather than the rays themselves. For students who have trouble understanding what an angle is, shading in the region between two rays is a helpful way to make an angle visible. Plus, this provides the opportunity to discuss that shading in a small corner vs. a wide swath does not change the size of the original angle.

4.5 Nix: $a^2 + b^2 = c^2$

Because:

The Pythagorean Theorem is a conditional statement, not an equation. If $a^2 + b^2 = c^2$ is the only way we reference this important theorem teachers ask, "What is c?" rather than, "What is the hypotenuse?" and students yell out the formula without any consideration for the type of triangle needed. Recently my precalculus students were proving $\sin^2(x) + \cos^2(x) = 1$ and I had a right triangle with sides labeled opposite, adjacent and hypotenuse on the board. They could not figure out how to write an equation from that information without the a, b and c.

Fix:

The Pythagorean Theorem states "If a triangle is right, then the sum of the squares of the legs is equal to the square of the hypotenuse." Students need to consider the conditions and use precise vocabulary. The full theorem is certainly a mouthful which is why $a^2 + b^2 = c^2$ is what sticks in students memories, but $\text{leg}^2 + \text{leg}^2 = \text{hypotenuse}^2$ is reasonable to remember. Using the words leg and hypotenuse also clues students in that if the triangle does not have a hypotenuse then the Pythagorean Theorem does not apply. To reinforce the idea that this is a conditional statement, have students consider the contrapositive: if $\text{leg}^2 + \text{leg}^2 \neq \text{hypotenuse}^2$, then the triangle is not right. If students try this relationship for both right and non-right triangles they will see why the condition is necessary.

4.6 Nix: The Angle of Inclination Is the Same as the Angle of Depression

Trick Explanation:
Just re-draw the picture so the angle is in the bottom right corner and it works every time!

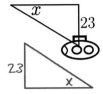

Because:

Students should not get in the habit of changing the diagram whenever they feel like it. If we want students to correctly interpret situations then they need to do so reliably. By drawing a new picture students also lose the understanding of what they are solving for. If the question asks for something in context, the student should give their answer in the original context. Depth and height are related but not the same. Not to mention that not all situations with angles of inclination or depression can be solved using right triangle trigonometry, so the angle will not always fall in the bottom right corner.

Fix:

These angles must be measured from something so have students start by drawing the horizontal. Then they can draw the angle of inclination or depression from the horizontal (going in the direction that corresponds to the word). Finally, drop a perpendicular somewhere useful based on the sketch and given information (assuming this is the right triangle trig unit, otherwise this trick did not apply in the first place!).

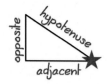

For students who struggle with identifying which is the opposite side and which is the adjacent side to the given angle, I have them first label the hypotenuse (the side opposite the right angle - which they do okay with) then cover the angle they are working with. The leg that they are not touching is the opposite side. The leg that they are touching is the adjacent side. No need to reorient the triangle!

Formulas

Frequently in geometry the lack of concept development comes from a different angle – formulas without background. These are not tricks, but if they are taught without context they become as magical as any other trick in this book. Formulas can be discovered, explored, derived or understood depending on the course, but if they are merely memorized they are no better than a meaningless shortcut. Giving students a formula without letting them experience the process takes away the thinking involved.

4.7 Formula: Areas of Quadrilaterals, Triangles

$$A = bh$$
$$A = \tfrac{1}{2}bh$$
$$A = lw$$
$$A = s^2$$

Understanding:

Start with $A = bh$ for rectangles. Students have seen arrays and may immediately make the connection to multiplication; for the other students, have them begin with rectangles having integer side lengths and count boxes. They will want a shortcut and can figure out that multiplying the side lengths will give the area. While length and width are perfectly acceptable names for the sides, base and height are more consistent with other shapes.

Next, explore how a parallelogram has the same area as a rectangle with equal base and height. Have students try some examples, then use decomposition to show that a right triangle can be cut from one end of the parallelogram and fit neatly onto the other end creating a rectangle. Thus, $A = bh$ for this shape as well!

Now is the time to look at triangles. I am always tempted (as are most students) to relate the area of a triangle to the area of a rectangle, but that connection only applies to right triangles. Allow students to see that *any* triangle is half of a parallelogram, thus: $A = \frac{1}{2}bh$.

And once they know the formula for a triangle, students can find the area of any two-dimensional figure by decomposition. Depending on the level, students could generalize their decompositions to find a simplified formula for familiar shapes such as trapezoids, but memorization of such formulas is unnecessary.

4.8 Formula: Surface Area

Understanding:

$$SA = 2bh + 2lb + 2lh$$
$$SA = 6s^2$$
$$LA = 2\pi rh$$

Many students do not realize that surface area is the sum of the areas of the faces of a shape. They may have been given a formula sheet with a box labeled Lateral Surface Area and another labeled Total Surface Area and played a matching game:

1. Find the key words (Section 2.1) in the question.

2. Match those to the words in the formula sheet.

3. Substitute numbers until the answer matches one of the choices provided.

Instead of playing the game, define surface area as the area of the surfaces. If students can identify the parts of the object (and have mastered 2-D area), then they can find the surface area. As a challenge task, ask students to draw

2-D nets that will fold into the object they are presented with. This is a practice in visualizing complex objects and understanding their connections to simpler objects. This sounds a lot like "Look for and make use of structure" a.k.a. Standard for Mathematical Practice 7 from the Common Core State Standards. The task of breaking down a cone or cylinder into its parts is one that is particularly difficult for students to do. Giving students paper nets to alternately build and flatten can help build intuition.

Depending on the level, students could generalize their process to find a simplified formula for familiar shapes such as rectangular prisms, but memorization of such formulas is unnecessary.

4.9   Formula: Volume

Understanding:

$$V = lbh$$
$$V = s^3$$
$$V = \pi r^2 h$$
$$V = \tfrac{1}{3}lwh$$

Just as surface area is the application of familiar area formulas to a new shape, volume formulas are not completely different for every shape, in fact they continue to apply familiar area formulas. There are two basic volume formulas: the prism and the pyramid. The prism formula is rather intuitive if students imagine stacking layers (or physically stack objects such as pattern blocks) they will realize that volume of a prism is the area of the base multiplied by the height. Once again, finding the value in question becomes a practice in visualizing – What is the base? How do I find its area? What is the height?

The formula for a pyramid is not as intuitive, but students can recognize that the area of a pyramid is less than the area of a prism with the same base and height. Some experimentation will show that the correct coefficient is $\frac{1}{3}$. This covers most shapes traditionally taught through high school (including cones as circular pyramids).

4.10 Formula: Distance Formula

Understanding: $$D = \sqrt{(y_2 - y_1)^2 + (x_2 - x_1)^2}$$

Please do not teach the distance formula before the Pythagorean Theorem! It is much harder for students to remember and does not provide any additional meaning. In my everyday life I only use the Pythagorean Theorem, nothing more. And as a math teacher, finding the distance between points is something I do somewhat regularly. Manipulating the Pythagorean Theorem to solve for different variables gives students practice solving equations. That said, it does not hurt students to see the distance formula somewhere in their mathematical career, so long as they see how it comes directly from the Pythagorean Theorem. The Pythagorean Theorem also gives us the equation for a circle; that one small formula turns out to be very powerful.

Chapter 5

Number Systems

5.1 Nix: Absolute Value Makes a Number Positive

$$| + 5| = +5$$

Because:

This is not a definition; this is an observation that follows from a definition. Additionally, this observation only applies to real numbers. Students are stuck when they need to solve equations using absolute value or when finding the absolute value of a complex number: $|4 - i| \neq 4 + i$.

Fix:

Geometrically, absolute value is the distance from zero. This definition is good for numbers and still holds for equations. When we move into two dimensions the slight tweak to "distance from the origin" is sufficient. Reinforce the fact that distance is positive through conversation (going five feet to the left is the same distance as going five feet to the right) or through the more formal algebraic definition of absolute value:

$$|x| = \begin{cases} -x & \text{for } x \leq 0 \\ x & \text{for } x \geq 0 \end{cases}$$

For $-x$ it is preferable to say 'the opposite of x' rather than 'negative x.'

5.2 Nix: Same-Change-Change, Keep-Change-Change (Integer Addition)

$$2 + (-5)$$
Keep Change Change
$$2 - (+5)$$

Because:

It has no meaning and there is no need for students to memorize a rule here. They are able to reason about adding integers (and extrapolate to the reals). A trick will circumvent thinking, while a tool like the number line will be a useful strategy throughout their studies.

$$100/(-2) = 100 \times (+2) = 200$$

http://mathmistakes.org/?p=328

This student takes Same-Change-Change and expands it to multiplication and division, presumably thinking "If you can magically switch between addition and subtraction, why not switch multiplication and division?"

Fix:

Once students are comfortable adding and subtracting whole numbers on the number line, all they need to add to their

44

previous understanding is that a negative number is the opposite of a positive number. There are many ways to talk about positive and negative numbers, but shifting on a number line is a good representation for students to be familiar with as this language will reappear during transformations of functions. Note: Some students may find a vertical number line (or even a representation of a thermometer) a more friendly tool to start with as up/down can be more intuitive than left/right.

$2 + 5$	Start at 2, move 5 spaces to the *right*
$2 + (-5)$	Start at 2, move 5 spaces to the *left* (opposite of right)
$2 - 5$	Start at 2, move 5 spaces to the *left*
$2 - (-5)$	Start at 2, move 5 spaces to the *right* (opposite of left)

5.3 Nix: Two Negatives Make a Positive (Integer Subtraction)

Because:

$$2 \overset{\frown}{\underset{2 + 5}{-}} 5$$

or

$$2 \overset{}{\underset{}{-\!\!+\!\!-}} 5$$

Again, it has no meaning and there is no need for students to memorize a rule here. Crossing out and changing signs makes students think that they can arbitrarily change the problem!

45

Fix:

The simplest approach here is to define subtraction as adding the opposite. An added bonus of changing from subtraction to addition is that addition is commutative!

As was the case in Section 5.2, students can reason through this on the number line. Once students recognize that addition and subtraction are opposites, and that positive and negative numbers are opposites, they will see that two opposites gets you back to the start. Just as turning around twice returns you to facing forward.

$$2 - (-5) \Rightarrow \text{Start at 2, move } (-5) \text{ spaces } down$$
$$\Rightarrow \text{Start at 2, move 5 spaces } up$$
$$\text{(opposite of down)}$$
$$\Rightarrow 2 + 5$$

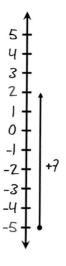

Therefore, $2 - (-5) = 2 + 5$. Make sure that when you are showing this to students (and when students do their work) that they show each of these steps separately. Otherwise, crossing out or changing symbols seems arbitrary when students refer to their notes.

Finally, students can see subtraction of integers as distance, just like they saw subtraction of whole numbers. Using a number line, start on the second number and move toward the first number. The direction tells you the sign and the number of spaces tells you the value.

5.4 Nix: Two Negatives Make a Positive (Integer Multiplication)

$$(-3)(-2) =$$
Because: $(+3)(+2) = +6$

Many students will overgeneralize and mistakenly apply this rule to addition as well as multiplication and division.

$$(-4)^{\oplus} - 7 = \,|\,|$$

http://mathmistakes.org/?p=328

For example, this student seems to be thinking: "Negative and negative = positive, right?"

Fix:

Students are able to reason about multiplying integers (and extrapolate to the reals) independently. They can look at patterns and generalize from a few approaches. One option is to use opposites:

> We know that $(3)(2) = 6$.
>
> So what should $(-3)(2)$ equal?
> The opposite of 6.
> Therefore, $(-3)(2) = -6$.
>
> And what should $(-3)(-2)$ equal?
> The opposite of -6.
> Therefore, $(-3)(-2) = 6$.

Another option is to use patterning. Since students are already familiar with the number line extending in both directions, they can continue to skip count their way right past zero into the negative integers.

Students can use the following pattern to determine that $(3)(-2) = -6$:

Product	Result
$(3)(2)$	6
$(3)(1)$	3
$(3)(0)$	0
$(3)(-1)$	-3
$(3)(-2)$	-6

With $(3)(-2) = -6$ in hand, students can use the following pattern to determine that $(-3)(-2) = 6$:

Product	Result
$(3)(-2)$	-6
$(2)(-2)$	-4
$(1)(-2)$	-2
$(0)(-2)$	0
$(-1)(-2)$	2
$(-2)(-2)$	4
$(-3)(-2)$	6

5.5 Nix: Move the Decimal (Scientific Notation)

Because:
$$6.25 \text{ x } 10^{-2} = {}_{\underset{\smile\smile}{.0\,6}}.25$$

Students get the answer right half the time and do not understand what went wrong the other half of the time. Students are thinking about moving the decimal place, not about place value or multiplying by 10.

Fix:

Students need to ask themselves, "Is this a big number or a small number?" Scientific notation gives us a compact way of writing long numbers, so is this long because it is large or long because it is small? An important idea of scientific notation is that you are not changing the value of the quantity, only its appearance. Writing a number in scientific notation is similar to factoring, but in this case we are only interested in factors of ten. Consider 6.25×10^{-2}: 10^{-2} is the reciprocal of 10^2 so

$$6.25 \times 10^{-2} = 6.25 \cdot \frac{1}{10^2} = \frac{6.25}{100} = .0625$$

To write 0.0289 in scientific notation, we need the first non-zero digit in the ones place; we need $2.89\times$ something. Compare 2.89 with 0.0289:

$$2.89 \times 10^x = 0.0289$$
$$\implies 10^x = \frac{0.0289}{2.89} = \frac{1}{100}$$
$$\implies x = -2$$

49

5.6 Nix: Jailbreak Radicals, aka You Need a Partner to Go to the Party

Trick Explanation:
The radical sign is a prison.

$$\sqrt{18} = \sqrt{3 \cdot 3} \cdot 2 = 3\sqrt{2}$$

The threes pair up and try to break out. Sadly, only one of them survives the escape.

Because:

It is one thing to tell a story; it is another for the story to have a mystery step where one number escapes and another disappears! This should not be a mystery. The second three did not disappear. When the square root operation was completed, 9 became 3, because 3 is the root of 9. Things happen for a reason, math makes sense.

Fix:

Show students how to identify perfect squares that are factors. We want them to rewrite the problem in a way that shows the math behind the magic:

$$\sqrt{18} = \sqrt{9 \cdot 2} = \sqrt{9} \cdot \sqrt{2} = 3\sqrt{2}$$

However, many students do not see perfect squares quickly or easily when factoring. There are two options here: one arithmetic and the other geometric.

Arithmetically, prime factorization helps students to find perfect squares, but they need to know what they are finding.

$$\sqrt{18} = \sqrt{2 \cdot 3 \cdot 3} = \sqrt{2 \cdot 3^2} = \sqrt{2} \cdot \sqrt{3^2} = 3\sqrt{2}$$

This approach reinforces that square and square root are inverse operations. Students know that $\sqrt{3^2} = 3$ by the definition of square root. Writing a prime factorization using exponents, then evaluating the square root on any perfect squares elucidates the process.

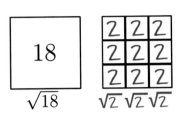

Geometrically, the square root function is asking for the side length of a square with given area. For $\sqrt{18}$ we are looking for the side length of a square with area 18 square units. One way to write that side length is $\sqrt{18}$ but there might be a simpler way to write that. What if we divided the square into nine smaller squares? Then the side length of each small square would be $\sqrt{2}$ and it takes three small sides to span one full side, thus $\sqrt{18} = 3\sqrt{2}$. When students engage in this process, they see the *squares* that are so important to finding a *square root*.

5.7 Nix: Exponent Over Radical

Because:

The entire fraction is an exponent, not just the numerator.

$$\underset{radical}{\overset{exponent}{}} \quad 3^{\frac{2}{5}} = \sqrt[5]{3^2}$$

Alphabetical:
e comes before r

Fix:

Describe exponents as indicating the number of factors of the base. So 2^3 is "three factors of two." This more clearly describes $2 \cdot 2 \cdot 2$ than the more typical "Two multiplied by itself three times" (that sounds like $((2 \cdot 2) \cdot 2) \cdot 2$). The bonus is that rational exponents fit this description.

$8^{\frac{1}{3}}$ means "One third of a factor of eight." as opposed to "Eight multiplied by it-self one third times." At first glance both phrases may seem equally nonsensical, but the first holds. To find a third of something you must break your whole into three equal parts, $8 = 2 \cdot 2 \cdot 2$, then you take one of them. Similarly, $16^{\frac{3}{4}}$ is "$\frac{3}{4}$ of a factor of 16." Break sixteen into four equal parts and take three of them.

$$8 = 2 \cdot 2 \cdot 2$$

$$8^{\frac{1}{3}} = 2$$

$$8^{\frac{2}{3}} = 2 \cdot 2 = 4$$

Students should still learn the connection between ra-tional exponents and radicals but this language allows the transition between whole number and fraction exponents to be a smooth one.

Chapter 6

Equations and Inequalities

6.1 Nix: 'Hungry' Inequality Symbols

$$3 \lessdot 5$$
$$4 \gtrdot 2$$

Because:

Students get confused with the alligator/pacman analogy. Is the bigger value eating the smaller one? Is it the value it already ate or the one it is about to eat?

Fix:

Ideally students have enough exposure to these symbols that they memorize the meaning. Just as they see and write $=$ when they hear or say "equal," students should see and write $<$ when they hear or say "less than." To help students before they internalize the meaning, have them analyze the shape. Instead of the segments being parallel like in an equal symbol, which has marks that are the same distance apart on both sides, the bars have been tilted to make a smaller side and a larger side. The greater number is next to the wider end and the lesser number is next to the narrower end. Beware of language here: use 'greater' rather than 'bigger' and 'less' rather than 'smaller.' When integers are brought into play, calling -5 'bigger' than -10 creates confusioin.

6.2 Nix: Take or Move to the Other Side

Because:

$$\boxed{-4}+ x = 12\ +4$$

Taking and moving are not algebraic operations. There are mathematical terms for what you are doing, attend to precision! When students think they can move things for any reason, they will neglect to use opposite operations.

$$2x + 3 = 3x - 4$$
$$5x + 3 = -4$$

http://mathmistakes.org/?p=517

Fix:

Using mathematical operations and properties to describe what we are doing will help students develop more precise language. Start solving equations using the utmost precision: "We add the opposite to each expression. That gives us $-4 + 4 = 0$ on the left and $12 + 4 = 16$ on the right."

$$x - 4 = 12$$
$$\underline{+4 = +4}$$
$$x + 0 = 16$$

This looks remarkably similar to solving a system of equations, because that is exactly what students are doing. We choose a convenient equation that will give us the additive identity (zero) to simplify that expression.

Similarly for multiplication and division, demonstrate: "If I divide each expression by three, that will give one on the right and a three in the denominator on the left."

$$\frac{-4}{3} = \frac{3x}{3}$$

$$\frac{-4}{3} = 1x$$

After time, students will be able to do some steps mentally and will omit the zero and the one in their written work, but they must be able to explain why the numbers disappeared. This is essential as when they reach more complex problems, the identities may need to remain for the equation to make sense. For example, the one might be all that remains of the numerator of a fraction – the denominator must be under *something*!

6.3 Nix: Switch the Side and Switch the Sign

Because:

$$\left(-4\right) + x = 12 + 4$$

This ditty hides the actual operation being used. Students who memorize a rhyme have no idea what they are doing. This leads to misapplication and the inability to generalize appropriately.

Fix:

Talk about inverse operations and getting to zero (in the case of addition) or one (in the case of multiplication) instead. The big idea is to maintain the equality by doing the same operation to both quantities.

6.4   Nix: Cancel

Because:

$$\frac{\cancel{5}x}{\cancel{5}} = 10$$

$$x = 10$$

Cancel is a vague term that hides the mathematical operations being used, so students do not know when or why to use it. To many students, cancel is digested as "cross-out stuff" by magic, so they see no problem with crossing out parts of an expression or across addition.

$$4x - 4(x + 2)$$
$$4x - \cancel{4}x + 8$$
$$+4x + \cancel{4}x$$
$$\overline{}$$
$$8x + 8$$

http://mathmistakes.org/?p=639

$$\frac{\cancel{\tan(x)}}{1 + \cancel{\sec(x)}} + \frac{1 + \cancel{\sec(x)}}{\cancel{\tan(x)}} = \frac{|}{|}$$

http://mathmistakes.org/?p=798

Fix:

Incorrect: $\dfrac{4x + 2}{2} = \dfrac{4x + \cancel{2}}{\cancel{2}} = 4x$

Correct: $\dfrac{4x + 2}{2} = \dfrac{\cancel{2}(2x + 1)}{\cancel{2}} = 2x$

Instead of saying cancel, require students to state a mathematical operation. Similarly, students should write a mathematical simplification rather than crossing out terms that 'cancel.' In fractions, we are dividing to get one.

Students can say "divides to one" and show that on their paper by making a big one instead of a slash to cross terms out. Alternately, students can circle the terms and write a one next to them. Emphasizing the division helps students see that they cannot cancel over addition (when students try to cross out part of the numerator with part of the denominator, for example).

When manipulating an equation, we are adding the opposite to each expression. Students can say "adds to zero" and show that on their paper by circling the terms and thinking of the circle as a zero or writing a zero next to them. In general, use the language of inverse operations, opposites and identities to precisely define the mysterious 'cancel.'

6.5 Nix: Follow the Arrow (Graphing Inequalities)

$$x \rightarrow 2$$

Because:

The inequalities $x > 2$ and $2 < x$ are equivalent and equally valid, yet they point in opposite directions. Plus, not all inequalities will be graphed on a horizontal number line!

Fix:

Students need to understand what the inequality symbol means. Ask students, "Are the solutions greater or lesser than the endpoint?" This is a great time to introduce test points – have students plot the endpoint, test a point in the inequality and then shade in the appropriate direction. While this seems like more work than knowing which direc-

57

tion to shade, it is a skill that applies throughout mathematics (including calculus!).

Since the symbolic representation of an inequality is more abstract than a number line, having students practice going from contexts or visual representations to symbolic ones will support student understanding of the symbols. While it is true that $x > 2$ is the more natural way to represent the sentence "the solutions are greater than two," students need the versatility of reading inequalities in both directions for compound inequalities. For example, $0 < x < 2$ requires students to consider both $0 < x$ and $x < 2$.

6.6 Nix: The Square Root and the Square Cancel

Because:
$$\sqrt{x^2} = x$$

Cancel is a vague term, it invokes the image of terms or operations magically disappearing. The goal is to make mathematics less about magic and more about reasoning. Something is happening here, let students see what is happening. Plus, the square root is only a *function* when you restrict the domain as the example below illustrates.

Fix:

Insist that students show each step instead of canceling operations.

$$\sqrt{(-5)^2} \neq -5 \text{ because } \sqrt{(-5)^2} = \sqrt{25} = 5$$

$$x^2 = 25 \quad \nRightarrow \quad x = \sqrt{25}$$

If you 'cancel' the square with a square root you miss a solution.

Instead:

$$\sqrt{x^2} = \sqrt{25} \quad \Leftrightarrow \quad |x| = \sqrt{25} \quad \Leftrightarrow \quad x = \pm\sqrt{25}$$

Another approach is to have students plot $y = \sqrt{x^2}$ and $y = (\sqrt{x})^2$ on their graphing utilities and compare results.

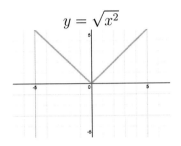

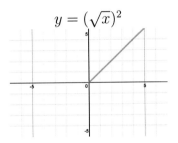

6.7   Nix: Land of Gor

Because:

$$|x| < 4 \qquad |x + 2| > 1$$

Besides the fact that this trick does not work when

Less → AND   Greater → OR
$-4 < x < 4$ $-1 < x + 2, \, x + 2 > 1$

the variable is on the right side of the inequality, the trick is unnecessary. This nonsensical phrase skips all the reasoning and understanding about absolute value inequalities. Students are capable of using the definiton of absolute value to figure out what type of inequality to write.

Fix:

Go back to the definition of absolute value (Section 5.1): $|x + 2| > d$ means "$x + 2$ is at a distance greater than d

units from zero." This distance can be both to the right of zero and to the left of zero, so students should recognize that an absolute value equation or inequality gives two options, one positive and one negative. The students should write out each of the inequalities separately, then use a graph or critical thinking to determine if the two parts can reasonably be merged into one compound inequality.

Placing the boxed expression above the number line reminds students that those are the endpoints for the expression, they still need to solve for the variable. Then listen to the language: if the inequality says $|x + 2| > d$ then we say "the distance is greater" so we shade the area farther from zero. In contrast, if the inequality says $|x + 2| < d$ then we say "the distance is less" so we shade the area closer to zero.

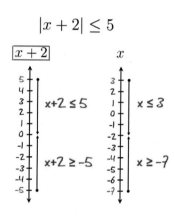

$$|x + 2| \leq 5$$

Since the number line is for $x + 2$, we subtract 2 from each expression in the inequalities to get the graph of x instead. This reinforces the idea that adding/subtracting shifts a graph. (It's also a nice place to show how dividing by a negative number flips the number line, which is why we have to change from > to < or vice versa.)

60

6.8 Nix: Log Circle

Because:

$$\log_a(b) = c \quad a^c = b$$

Students taught to go around the circle do not understand what a log is nor what it does.

Fix:

Go back to the definition of a logarithm. Every time students see a log they should remember that $\log_a(b)$ asks the question: "What exponent is required for a base of a to reach a value of b?" If students continually refer back to that question, they will be able to both rewrite a log in exponential form and know what the logarithm function means. The log has two inputs – the value and the base – and gives an output of the exponent, or, in the language of Section 5.7, the log outputs the number of factors.

6.9 Nix: The Log and the Exponent Cancel

Because:

$$2^{\log_2 x} = X$$

Cancel is a vague term, it invokes the image of terms or operations magically disappearing. The goal is to make mathematics less about magic and more about reasoning. Something is happening here, let students see what is happening!

$$\log_2 x = 4$$

$$2^{\log_2 x} = 2^4$$

$$x = 2^4$$

If you know the definition of a log the second line is unnecessary. There is no reason to be cancelling anything, the simplest approach is to rewrite the equation using knowledge of logs.

If students are not thinking about the definition of a log, they will try to solve the new function in the ways they are familiar with.

One student divides by the function:
$$2log(6x) - log(9) = log(36)$$

$$\frac{log}{log\ 6x} \quad \frac{log}{-\ 9} \quad \frac{log}{=\ 36}$$

$$log\ 6x = 45$$

http://mathmistakes.org/?p=95

Another student divides by the base:
$$ln(4) + ln(6x) = ln(48)$$

$$\frac{e}{4} \quad + \quad \frac{e}{6x} \quad \frac{e}{=\ 48}$$

$$6x \quad = 44$$

$$x \quad = 7.4$$

http://mathmistakes.org/?p=67

62

Fix:

Rewrite the log in exponent form, then solve using familiar methods. This is another reason to teach the definition of logarithms; then there is no confusion about the relationship between logs and exponents.

The log asks the question *"base* to what *power* equals *value?"*

$$\log_{base} value = power$$
$$base^{power} = value$$

$$\log_2 8 = y$$
$$2^y = 8$$
$$y = 3$$

$$\log_2 x = 4$$
$$2^4 = x$$
$$16 = x$$

Chapter 7

Functions

7.1 Nix: Rise over Run as the Definition of Slope

Because:

Slope is a very important concept and it needs a robust definition. 'Rise over run' can describe how to find slope in a graph, but slope has a deeper meaning than counting boxes. Additionally, some students think 'rise' means you are always going up, which causes problems.

Fix:

Slope is the rate of change. Students can find that rate by comparing the change in y (or y-distance) to the change in x (or x-distance). When students are computing slope they are finding the rate of something per something else. Starting with a context (for example, rate of students per hour) is helpful to provide a foundation for understanding, but this phrasing holds in all cases, even if it means saying rate of y per each x.

Begin by analyzing slope as how much y changes each time that x changes by one, but do not leave that as the only option. The slope in $y = mx + b$ tells students 'for any change in x, y changes by m times as much." For example, "If I change x by one, y changes by m." is true, but the statement "If I change x by $\frac{7}{3}$, y changes by $m \cdot \frac{7}{3}$" is equally true.

The benefit of this definition is that students can recognize slope from a table (even if the x-difference is not one), a word problem and a graph.

7.2   Nix: OK vs. NO Slope

$$\frac{N}{O} \quad \frac{O}{K}$$

Because:

What is the difference between "no slope" and "zero slope?" Students frequently confuse 'no solution' with 'the solution is zero' and this trick does not help students to tell the difference.

Fix:

Slope can be negative, positive, zero or *undefined*. If students struggle to remember that dividing by zero is undefined, have them go back to multiplication and fact families. We know $\frac{10}{2} = 5$ because $10 = 5 \cdot 2$. Now try that with zero in the denominator. $\frac{10}{0} = a$ means $10 = a \cdot 0$. There are no values of a which make that true. On the other hand, $\frac{0}{10} = b$ means $0 = b \cdot 10$. In this case there is a solution, $b = 0$. Once students have seen why dividing by zero is undefined, do a google image search for "divide by zero" and enjoy a laugh (you might want to turn on safe search, there are some with inappropriate language). If you or the students are interested in further exploration, try some values getting close to zero.

$$\frac{10}{1} = 10$$

$$\frac{10}{.1} = 100$$

$$\frac{10}{.01} = 1000$$

Imagine what would happen as the denominator gets closer and closer to zero. What is the limit?

7.3 Nix: What is b?

Because: $$y = mx + \boxed{b}$$

The answer to this question is, "b is a letter." It does not have any inherent meaning; instead ask students exactly what you are looking for, which is probably either the y-intercept or a point to use when graphing the line.

Fix:

There are many equations of a line, $y = mx + b$ is just one of them. In fact, it is not necessarily written that way depending on what country or system you are in. Given the goal of graphing, feel free to ask what the intercept of the line is, but it is much easier to ask for any point. Have students pick a value for x (eventually they will gravitate toward zero anyway since it is easy to multiply by!) and then solve for y. This method works for any equation and it shows why we put the value of b on the y-axis. Remind students that, while b is a number, we are concerned with $(0, b)$ which is a point.

7.4   Nix: The Inside Does the Opposite

Because:

You are telling students that the truth is the opposite of their intuition. This assumes you know their intuition, and it certainly does not help with sense making to say this makes the opposite of sense! Remember, math makes sense.

$$\overset{\text{stretch}}{\underset{\underset{\text{stretch}}{\text{un-}}}{a}} \cdot f(\underset{\underset{\text{shift}}{\text{negative}}}{bx + c}) \overset{\underset{\text{shift}}{\text{positive}}}{+d}$$

Fix:

Show students what transformations are happening by showing – algebraically as well as graphically – how to transform the parent function into the equation. Any time we get to use change of variable you know students are practicing seeing structure in expressions (an important Common Core Strand). The benefit of these particular variables is we can say I is for input and O is for output.

$$y = (x - 5)^2 - 7$$
$$y + 7 = (x - 5)^2$$
$$O = I^2$$

Now students can take the values of the parent function and transform them accordingly to graph the original equation.

I	O
-2	4
-1	1
0	0
1	1
2	4

x	I	O	y
3	-2	4	-3
4	-1	1	-6
5	0	0	-7
6	1	1	-6
7	2	4	-3

$$I = x - 5$$
$$x = I + 5 \text{ Shift right 5.}$$
$$O = y + 7$$
$$y = O - 7 \text{ Shift down 7.}$$

This is a convenient way to sketch a graph since if students know the important points in a parent function (vertex, maximum, minimum), they will get those same important points on their graph! It works for shifts and stretches as well as any type of functions (including trig, which is awesome since students struggle to find x values that they even know the sine of when making a table).

When I first taught Algebra 1, I had students graph quadratics by making a table and used the integers between -5 and 5 for x every time. This worked fine for the functions I gave them, but when they got to Algebra 2 their teacher reported back to me that not all graphs had a vertex with $-5 \leq x \leq 5$ and my former students were stuck on what to do when their graph did not look like the parabola they expected to see. Sorry first year students, if I had only had that professional development day with the Educational Development Center sooner!

7.5 Nix: All Students Take Calculus a.k.a CAST

Because:

$$\begin{array}{c|c} Sin & All \\ \hline Tan & Cos \end{array}$$

Students do not need a rule to figure out which trig functions are positive in each quadrant. Why add an extra layer of memorization? Especially when it is not even true that all students take calculus!

Fix:

Think. If a student is studying trigonometry they know that right is positive and left is negative on the x-axis. Similarly, they know that up is positive and down is negative on the y-axis. Finally, students know how to divide integers (or they will once you share Section 5.4 with them). These three simple facts are all it takes to identify if a function is positive or negative in that quadrant, and most students find all three of those automatic by this point in their mathematical careers. But, more importantly, we should not be askng students to only find the sign of a trig function in a quadrant. Instead ask them to find the value of a function. Using the coordinates from the unit circle for the given angle eliminates the need for any memorization.

7.6 Nix: FOIL

Because:

FOIL only applies to multiplying two binomials, a very specific task. There are other ways to multiply binomials that come

$$(2x + 3)(x - 4)$$

First   Inside

$$2x^2 - 8x + 3x - 12$$

Outside   Last

from simpler distribution problems and are transferrable to later work such as multiplying larger polynomials and factoring by grouping. It also implies an order – a few of my honors precalculus students were shocked to learn that OLIF works just as well as FOIL does.

When students memorize a rule without understanding they misapply it.

$$(a+3)(a+3) = 2a + 6$$

http://mathmistakes.org/?p=1180

$$(7k+2)(5k-8)$$
$$12K - 6$$
$$-12K + 6$$

http://mathmistakes.org/?p=1100

Fix:

Replace FOIL with the distributive property. It can be taught as soon as distribution is introduced. Students can start by distributing one binomial to each part of the other binomial. Then distribution is repeated on each monomial being multiplied by a binomial. As students repeat the procedure they will realize that each term in the first polynomial must be multiplied by each term in the second polynomial. This pattern, which you might term "each by each" carries through the more advanced versions of this exercise.

In elementary school students learn an array model for multiplying numbers. The box method builds on this knowledge of partial products.

$$23 \cdot 45 = (20 + 3)(40 + 5)$$
$$= 20(40 + 5) + 3(40 + 5)$$
$$= 20 \cdot 40 + 20 \cdot 5 + 3 \cdot 40 + 3 \cdot 5$$
$$= 800 + 100 + 120 + 15$$

	40	**5**
20	800	100
3	120	15

$$(2x + 3)(x - 4)$$
$$= (2x + 3)(x) + (2x + 3)(-4)$$
$$= 2x^2 + 3x - 8x - 12$$
$$= 2x^2 - 5x - 12$$

	2x	**3**
x	$2x^2$	$3x$
−4	$-8x$	-12

7.7 Nix: Slide and Divide, aka Throw the Football

Because:

$$2x^2 - 5x - 12$$
$$\underset{slide}{\underleftarrow{\qquad\qquad}}$$

The middle steps are not equivalent to the original expression so students cannot switch to an alternate method partway through. Either students are led to believe that $2x^2 - 5x - 12 = x^2 - 5x - 24$

$x^2 - 5x - 24$
$(x - 8)(x + 3)$
now divide:
$(x - 8/2)(x + 3/2)$
$(x - 4)(2x + 3)$

(which is false) or they know it is not equal and they are forced to blindly trust that the false equivalence will somehow result in a correct answer. Do not ask for students' faith, show them that math makes sense.

Fix:

This trick is not so far off from a great way to factor using chunking. Consider the trinomial $4x^2 - 10x - 24$. The first term is a perfect square, so I could use some substitution where $a = 2x$ and get $4x^2 - 10x - 24 = a^2 - 5a - 24$. This is a monic expression so it is easier to factor. Then I can substitute $a = 2x$ back in to get the solution to my original expression.

$$\begin{aligned}
4x^2 - 10x - 24 &= a^2 - 5a - 24 \\
&= (a - 8)(a + 3) \\
&= (2x - 8)(2x + 3)
\end{aligned}$$

You may be thinking, this is all well and good, but what do I do when the first term is not a perfect square? That's what this trick is doing – without showing you the structure – it is making the first term a perfect square for you. If we want to factor $2x^2 - 5x - 12$, the first term needs another factor of two. Now, this will change the value of the expression, but it is a temporary change and we are going to make it obvious that we have changed it, no blind trust:

$$2(2x^2 - 5x - 12) = 4x^2 - 10x - 24$$
$$= a^2 - 5a - 24, \text{ where } a = 2x$$
$$= (a - 8)(a + 3)$$
$$= (2x - 8)(2x + 3)$$
$$= 2(x - 4)(2x + 3)$$

So we know that $2(2x^2 - 5x - 12) = 2(x - 4)(2x + 3)$, thus $2x^2 - 5x - 12 = (x - 4)(2x + 3)$. We factored that trinomial! (Remember - this method works because the problem was rigged to be factorable. If the original trinomial is not factorable things will not fall out so nicely.)

So, now that we know why this trick works, is it worth using? I think this method is a nice way to have students practice seeing structure in expressions (an important Common Core Strand), if they start with monics, move to quadratics with perfect squares and finally see this process. Many teachers were raised on 'guess and check' factoring, and were pretty good at it – but many students struggle with that method. The box method (equivalent to factoring by parts) can help students to organize their information.

(1)	$\_\_x$	
$\_\_x$	$2x^2$	$\_\_x$
	$\_\_x$	-12

(2)	$2x$	
$1x$	$2x^2$	$\_\_x$
	$\_\_x$	-12

(3)	$2x$	2
$1x$	$2x^2$	$\_\_x$
-6	$\_\_x$	-12

(1) Fill in the box just like for multiplying polynomials (Section 7.6)

(2) The only factors of 2 are 2 and 1, so fill in those boxes.

(3) Try 2 and -6 as the factors of -12.

(4)	$2x$	2
$1x$	$2x^2$	$2x$
-6	$-12x$	-12

(5)	$2x$	3
$1x$	$2x^2$	$\_\_x$
-4	$\_\_x$	-12

(6)	$2x$	3
$1x$	$2x^2$	$3x$
-4	$-8x$	-12

(4) The coefficient of x was supposed to be -5 but $2x - 12x = -10x$

(5) Try again, this time using 3 and -4 as the factors of -12.

(6) Success! $3x - 8x = -5x$ The factorization is $(2x + 3)(1x - 4)$.

There is something to be said for practicing factoring integers but it will depend on the student and the goals. Completing the square and the quadratic formula are lovely methods that work for all quadratics. The methods a student learns will depend on their level. It is better to have a variety of options when teaching, but that does not mean that every student needs to learn every option.

7.8 Nix: Synthetic Division

Because:

$$(x^3 - 6x^2 + 7x + 6)/(x - 3)$$

Students do not know when synthetic division works or why it works. The goal is

$$\underline{3}\,\lfloor\,1\ -6\ \ 7\ \ 6$$
$$3\ \ 9\ -6$$
$$\overline{\,1\ \ 3\ -2\,\lfloor 0}$$

$|x^2 - 3x - 2$

to divide quickly, but using a graphing utility or computer algebra system is even faster! It is more important for students to understand the process and how to interpret an answer. Once students achieve this, then the algorithm can be carried out by a computer. Besides, the way synthetic division is usually taught only works for the limitied case of a polynomial divided by $(x - a)$ (it is possible to modify the process for any polynomial but it is rare to see that approach in school).

Fix:

Use polynomial long division exclusively for showing students how to solve by hand. Students can make the connection between polynomials and real numbers to see that the process is equivalent. Once students understand the process and why it works, use technology for everything else. Cool fact – the long division process highlighted in Section 2.6 works just as well for polynomials as it does for numbers!

$$
\begin{array}{r}
7 \\
10 \\
100
\end{array}\Big\} \, 117\,R4
$$

$$
\begin{array}{r}
7\,\overline{)823} \\
-700 \\
\hline
123 \\
-\;70 \\
\hline
53 \\
-\;49 \\
\hline
4
\end{array}
$$

$$
\begin{array}{r}
x^2 - 3x - 2 \\
x - 3\,\overline{)x^3 - 6x^2 + 7x + 6} \\
-\,(x^3 - 3x^2) \\
\hline
-3x^2 + 7x + 6 \\
-\,(-3x^2 + 9x) \\
\hline
-2x + 6 \\
-\,(-2x + 6) \\
\hline
0
\end{array}
$$

Chapter 8

Conclusion

"Okay, I've read the book and I want to Nix the Tricks. Now what?"

Start slowly. High school teacher Jonathan Claydon, who blogs at InfiniteSums.com, recommends picking just two tricks this year. Go back through the book, decide which tricks come up the most often in your class or which concepts will provide the best foundation for your students as they continue learning mathematics. Then make a promise to try your very best to never use those phrases. One trick I'm still working on nixing is Cancel (Section 6.4). We solve equations using opposite operations all the time in my precalculus class and both my language and my students' language defaults to 'cancel.' Sometimes I catch myself before the word comes out of my mouth and I congratulate myself, then say the precise operation. Other times I say 'cancel,' silently curse myself, then silently forgive myself and finally follow the imprecise language with a precise statement. Most of the time students tell me to cancel something and I ask them how or narrate my thought process as

I record the opposite operations. It takes many repetitions to undo a habit that has been ingrained in students for a long time, and in me for at least twice as long!

"What about the kids who already know a trick?"

Step one, hand a copy of this book to the teacher, tutor or parent who taught it to them. (I am only sort of kidding.) Step two, engage the students in some sense-making. Can they explain the math behind the trick? If so, it really only counts as a shortcut, not a trick, since they understand the math. Even so, it may trip them up later, so ask about some situations where it applies and does not apply. Push students to see if it is the most efficient method in a variety of situations. Any question you can ask to get students thinking rather than blindly obeying a rule is a great idea.

Middle school math teacher David Cox, who blogs at CoxMath.blogspot.com had a brilliant response when his students told him an assignment was easy since they just use the DRT triangle (Section 3.10). First, he asked them what it was and how it worked. Then, he told them that he had learned the TRD triangle. The students responded with conflicting statements.

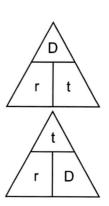

S_1: "No, that won't work. That's not what he told us."

S_2 : "He said it didn't matter how we wrote it."

Mr. Cox: "So which is it; does one work or are they the same? Make your case and be ready to defend it."

To decide if the new triangle worked (and the old one for that matter!) the students tried some examples that they understood without needing the triangle. They generated their own problems, drew conclusions and formed an argument. Any day where students use something they understand to reason about something new is a great day for mathematics. Find the complete story on David's blog: http://coxmath.blogspot.com/2014/04/dirty-triangles.html

"Will my middle schoolers/high schoolers/college students really buy into this after learning math with tricks for so long?"

Yes! Some of my high school students are still curious enough to ask me why a method that they were told to take on faith works. Other students exclaim, "Ooohh! That's why we do that." when I show them something in a new way. I truly believe that every student would rather understand than memorize a list of steps, but some students are resistant because they fear that they are not smart enough to do math.

Don't take my word for it though, other people are seeing success using Nix the Tricks:

Justin Aion
Middle School Teacher
http://relearningtoteach.blogspot.com/

> Day 120:
> I think I have successfully cured my pre-algebra students of using "cross-multiply." When we started proportions, I heard it with every other problem. Now, I don't think I've heard it in over a week. What I'm hearing instead is "don't we multiply 15 to both sides?"

> Day 143:
> After we completed the 8 word problems, I asked a simple question:
> Me: "What did I not see in any of these problems? What tactic was not used?"
> S: "Cross-multiplication."
> Me: "Did anyone even think to use it?"
> S: **silence**

> YES!!! One trick nixed!

Jonathan Claydon
High School Teacher
http://infinitesums.com/commentary/2014/3/23/nixing-tricks

> I set two goals: never say "cancel" and never say "cross multiply." Try as hard as possible to prevent the students from saying those words either. If I force them to be proper about it early the growing pains will be worth it.

> Every time we needed to clear a denominator I showed it as an operation of multiplying both sides by the relevant terms. Every time we took a square root I mentioned the presence of two solutions. Forcing myself to rely on the mathematically valid reasoning slowly influenced the students. They raised the level at which they explained concepts to each other. I didn't hear anyone looking for an easy way out. They wanted to do it *my* way.

> This process became cyclical. As I saw my students rise to the challenge, I felt an obligation to them and the professional community to continue to focus on valid, universal mathematical explanations for things.

To share your own stories of success or struggle with nixing tricks, visit NixTheTricks.com. While you are there explore additional resources (videos, relevant research and more!) and contribute to the sections in development. This is a community project that exists due to the efforts of many people, join us in pushing it to become an ever more comprehensive and helpful compilation.

Appendix A

Index of Tricks by Standards

Sorted by the Common Core State Standards.

1.OA.A.2	Section 2.1 Total Means Add
2.NBT.B.9	Section 2.2 Bigger Bottom, Better Borrow
3.MD.D.8	Section 4.1 Perimeter is the Outside
3.G.A.1	Section 4.2 Rectangles Have Two Long Sides and Two Short Sides
3.G.A.1	Section 4.3 Squares Have Four Equal Sides
3.OA.B.5	Section 2.3 Add a Zero (Multiplying by 10)
3.NBT.A.1	Section 2.4 Five or More Go up a Floor, aka 0-4 Hit the Floor, 5-9 Make the Climb
4.G.A.1	Section 4.4 Obtuse Angles are Big
4.MD.A.3	Section 4.7 Area of Quadrilaterals, Triangles
4.NBT.A.2	Section 6.1 'Hungry' Inequality Symbols
4.NBT.B.5	Section 2.5 Turtle Multiplication
4.NBT.B.6	Section 2.6 Does McDonald's Sell Cheeseburgers, aka Dad, Mom, Sister, Brother
5.OA.A.1	Section 2.8 PEMDAS, BIDMAS
5.NBT.B.7	Section 2.7 Ball to the Wall
5.NF.A.1	Section 3.1 Butterfly Method, Jesus Fish
5.NF.B.3	Section 3.2 The Man on the Horse
5.NF.B.3	Section 3.3 Make Mixed Numbers MAD
5.NF.B.3	Section 3.4 Backflip and Cartwheel
6.EE.B.7	Section 6.2 Take/Move to the Other Side
6.EE.B.7	Section 6.3 Switch the Side, Switch the Sign
6.NS.A.1	Section 3.5 Cross Multiply (Fraction Division)
6.NS.A.1	Section 3.6 Flip and Multiply, Same-Change-Flip

6.NS.C.7   Section 5.1 Absolute Value Makes
           a Number Positive
6.RP.A.3   Section 3.8 Dr. Pepper
6.RP.A.3   Section 3.9 New Formulas for
           Each Conversion
6.RP.A.3   Section 3.10 Formula Triangle
7.EE.B.4   Section 6.5 Follow the Arrow
           (Graphing Inequalities)
7.G.B.6   Section 4.8 Surface Area
7.G.B.6   Section 4.9 Volume
7.NS.A.1   Section 5.2 Same-Change-Change,
           Keep-Change-Change
7.NS.A.1   Section 5.3 Two Negatives Make a
           Positive (Integer Subtraction)
7.NS.A.2   Section 5.4 Two Negatives Make a
           Positive (Integer Multiplication)
7.NS.A.2   Section 7.2 OK vs. NO Slope
7.RP.A.3   Section 3.7 Cross Multiply
           (Solving Proportions)

8.EE.A.2   Section 6.6 The Square Root and
           the Square Cancel
8.EE.A.4   Section 5.5 Move the Decimal
           (Scientific Notation)
8.EE.B.5   Section 7.1 Rise over Run as the
           Definition of Slope
8.F.A.3   Section 7.3 What is b?
8.G.B.7   Section 4.5 $a^2 + b^2 = c^2$
8.G.B.8   Section 4.10 Distance Formula

A-APR.D.6	Section 3.11 Outers over Inners
A-APR.D.6	Section 7.8 Synthetic Division
A-REI.B.3	Section 6.7 Land of Gor
A-REI.B.4	Section 6.8 Slide and Divide, aka Throw the Football
A-SSE.A.2	Section 7.6 FOIL
F-BF.B.5	Section 6.8 Log Circle
F-BF.B.5	Section 6.9 The Log and the Exponent Cancel
F-IF.C.7	Section 7.4 The Inside Does the Opposite
F-TF.A.2	Section 7.5 All Students Take Calculus
G-SRT.C.8	Section 4.6 The Angle of Inclination Is the Same as the Angle of Depression
N-RN.A.2	Section 5.6 Jailbreak Radicals, aka You Need a Partner to Go to the Party
N-RN.A.2	Section 5.7 Exponent Over Radical
SMP 6	Section 6.4 Cancel

Appendix B

Types of Tricks

B.1 Imprecise Language

Section 4.1 Perimeter is the Outside
Section 4.2 Rectangles Have Two Long Sides and Two Short Sides
Section 4.3 Squares Have Four Equal Sides
Section 4.4 Obtuse Angles are Big
Section 5.1 Absolute Value Makes a Number Positive
Section 7.2 OK vs. NO Slope
Section 6.6 The Square Root and the Square Cancel
Section 7.1 Rise over Run as the Definition of Slope
Section 4.5 $a^2 + b^2 = c^2$
Section 6.9 The Log and the Exponent Cancel
Section 6.4 Cancel

B.2 Methods Eliminating Options

Section 3.8 Dr. Pepper
Section 3.9 New Formulas for Each Conversion
Section 3.10 Formula Triangle
Section 3.7 Cross Multiply (Solving Proportions)
Section 7.3 What is b?
Section 4.10 Distance Formula
Section 7.6 FOIL

B.3 Tricks Students Misinterpret

Section 6.1 'Hungry' Inequality Symbols
Section 2.8 PEMDAS, BIDMAS
Section 3.2 The Man on the Horse
Section 3.5 Cross Multiply (Fraction Division)
Section 3.6 Flip and Multiply, Same-Change-Flip
Section 6.5 Follow the Arrow (Graphing Inequalities)
Section 5.3 Two Negatives Make a Positive (Integer Subtraction)
Section 5.4 Two Negatives Make a Positive (Integer Multiplication)
Section 3.11 Outers over Inners

B.4 Math as Magic, Not Logic

Section 2.1 Total Means Add
Section 2.2 Bigger Bottom, Better Borrow
Section 2.3 Add a Zero (Multiplying by 10)
Section 2.4 Five or More Go up a Floor, aka 0-4 Hit the Floor, 5-9 Make the Climb
Section 2.5 Turtle Multiplication
Section 2.6 Does McDonald's Sell Cheeseburgers, aka Dad, Mom, Sister, Brother
Section 2.7 Ball to the Wall
Section 3.1 Butterfly Method, Jesus Fish
Section 3.3 Make Mixed Numbers MAD
Section 3.4 Backflip and Cartwheel
Section 6.2 Take/Move to the Other Side
Section 6.3 Switch the Side, Switch the Sign
Section 5.2 Same-Change-Change, Keep-Change-Change
Section 5.5 Move the Decimal (Scientific Notation)
Section 7.8 Synthetic Division
Section 6.7 Land of Gor
Section 7.7 Slide and Divide, aka Throw the Football
Section 6.8 Log Circle
Section 7.4 The Inside Does the Opposite
Section 7.5 All Students Take Calculus
Section 4.6 The Angle of Inclination Is the Same as the Angle of Depression
Section 5.6 Jailbreak Radicals, aka You Need a Partner to Go to the Party
Section 5.7 Exponent Over Radical

Made in the USA
Middletown, DE
27 January 2018